Rookie choices®

THE BIG TEE BALL GAME

THE CORNER KIDS

Written by Larry Dane Brimner • Illustrated by Christine Tripp

Children's Press®
A Division of Scholastic Inc.
New York • Toronto • London • Auckland • Sydney
Mexico City • New Delhi • Hong Kong
Danbury, Connecticut

For Neal and Joan Broerman
—L.D.B.

For my daughter Emily
—C.T.

Reading Consultants
Linda Cornwell
Coordinator of School Quality and Professional Improvement
(Indiana State Teachers Association)

Katharine A. Kane
Education Consultant
(Retired, San Diego County Office of Education and San Diego State University)

Library of Congress Cataloging-in-Publication Data

Brimner, Larry Dane.
    The big tee ball game / by Larry Dane Brimner; illustrated by Christine Tripp.
        p. cm. — (Rookie choices)
    Summary: Gabby discovers that cheating at tee ball is not the best way to win.
    ISBN 0-516-22158-2 (lib. bdg.)   0-516-25974-1 (pbk.)
    [1. Cheating—Fiction. 2. Winning and Losing—Fiction 3. Sportsmanship—Fiction.
4. T-ball—Fiction.] I. Tripp, Christine, ill. II. Title. III. Series.
PZ7.B767 Bk 2001
[E]—dc21   00-047562

This book is about **sportsmanship**.

It was the last inning,
and the score was tied.
The Corner Kids—Gabby,
Three J, and Alex—were on
their way to the field with the
rest of their team, the Bobcats.

"We can't let them score," said Three J

"Just once I'd like to beat the Cubs."

"Don't worry,"
Gabby said.

"But the Cubs have won every game they've played," Alex said.

Gabby shrugged and smiled, as if she knew something the others didn't.

Three Cubs came to bat.
Three Cubs struck out.

Even when they had hit the ball,
it had not flown off the tee.

Now it was the Bobcats' turn
to bat. They jogged toward
the backstop.

"One run," said Alex.
"That's all we need to win."

Gabby didn't say anything,
but when she passed the tee,
she pulled hard on the ball.

Pop!

She picked another one from
the basket and placed it on the
tee instead.

Three J was on third base by the
time Gabby stepped up to bat.
"One run," she told herself, but
it made her stomach do flip-flops
when she did.

She swung the bat, and Three J raced
toward home plate.

19

Later, the Bobcats lifted Three J, Gabby, and the winners' cup into the air.

"Wait!" Gabby said. She looked
around at all the happy faces.
"Put me down. I'm sorry."
Her voice became a whisper.
"We didn't win."

Everyone looked confused.

23

"I put gum under the ball,"
Gabby said. "That's why the Cubs
didn't get any hits. I thought
winning would feel good, but . . . "
Gabby handed the cup to the
Cubs' captain.

Everyone was
quiet then,
even the Cubs.

On the way home, the Corner Kids didn't talk until Three J spoke up.

"Telling what you did was brave," he said to Gabby.

"It was," Alex agreed, and then he tried to make her smile. "Hey, Gabby," he said. "Do you know why the batter didn't dance with Cinderella?"

Gabby shrugged.

"He missed the ball."

They all laughed at that.

Then Gabby became serious.
"We don't need to cheat to win,"
she said. "Next year we'll win by
the rules."

31

ABOUT THE AUTHOR

Larry Dane Brimner studied literatur and writing at San Diego Stat University and taught school f twenty years. The author of more tha seventy-five books for children, mar of them Children's Press titles, h enjoys meeting young readers an writers when he isn't at his compute

ABOUT THE ILLUSTRATOR

Christine Tripp lives in Ottawa, Canada, with her husband Don; four grown children—Elizabeth, Erin, Emily, and Eric; son-in-law Jason; grandsons Brandon and Kobe; four cats; and one very large, scruffy puppy named Jake.